Loving Together

Sexual Enrichment Program

by

Lonnie Barbach, Ph.D.

DISCOVERING ORGASM WORKBOOK

ISBN: 87630-857-4 Discovering Orgasm Workbook

ISBN: 87630-854-X Sexual Desire Workbook
ISBN: 87630-856-6 Erection Control Workbook
ISBN: 87630-855-8 Ejaculation Control Workbook
ISBN: 87630-853-1 Therapist's Manual

Published by
BRUNNER/MAZEL, INC.
A member of the Taylor & Francis Group
1900 Frost Road, Suite 101
Bristol, Pennsylvania 19007

Manufactured in the United States of America

10 9 8 7 6 5 4 3 2 1

TABLE OF CONTENTS

INTRODUCTION

Every woman is preorgasmic at some time in her life. We all have to learn to have orgasms. For some women, this learning process is more difficult than for others and obstacles can arise from a variety of different sources. But, in general, the solution is the same: You need to learn about your own sexual preferences and areas of sexual sensitivity through self-stimulation. As you learn to experience orgasm on your own, you then have information to share with your partner and ways to expand the activities that offer pleasure during partner sex.

Some of the early exercises in this program are designed to help those of you who have received very negative messages during your childhoods, either from your families or your religions. These exercises can help you learn to appreciate the life affirming and positive aspects of sexuality. If you have been sexually abused, you may require additional therapy to help you deal with the trauma of the abuse before you may be able to approach the issues of sex and orgasm successfully.

While orgasm is the skill being taught in this program, the real goal is to allow you to experience sexual pleasure fully and without inhibition. Orgasm is the end result of the build-up of sexual pleasure. So, rather than focusing on orgasm, the orientation of this program will be for you to learn to build sexual pleasure. For most women, when pleasurable feelings are thoroughly enjoyed and sustained, orgasm occurs without much difficulty. However, it is unreasonable for most women to expect to reach orgasm every time they have sex. There may be occasions when you feel too tired or just not sufficiently turned-on to reach orgasm, but you can still enjoy the comfort, sensuality, and intimacy that sexual contact offers. At other times, unresolved conflict will need to be addressed before you can expect your sexual feelings to open up.

Most women will not experience orgasm without some form of direct clitoral stimulation. This means that to attain orgasm during intercourse, you will need to have additional clitoral stimulation either from intercourse positions where your clitoris is being stimulated by your partner's pubic bone or by you or your partner manually stimulating your clitoris during intercourse.

The Loving Together: Discovering Orgasm Program consists of 12 weeks of exercises that will teach you in a step-by-step fashion to experience orgasm with your partner.

Some of the necessary skills will be taught first through masturbation. Afterward, partner exercises will be outlined so you can transfer the skills to lovemaking with your mate. The masturbation exercises have been divided up into 5 categories.

Follow the exercises labeled (A), (B), (C), (D), or (E) depending on the following criteria.

(A) If you are unable to masturbate to orgasm using your hands

(B) If you are reliably orgasmic with manual masturbation, but never or rarely with partner sex

(C) If you have been orgasmic with a previous partner, but not with your current partner

(D) If you used to be orgasmic with your current partner, but are not any longer

(E) If you are inconsistently orgasmic with your partner

Since no sexual difficulty can be considered in a vacuum, weekly exercises have been included to enhance the level of communication and positive feeling toward your partner. While these exercises form the foundation for intimacy outside the bedroom, they affect sexual satisfaction as well. There are also exercises that deal with increasing your awareness of pleasure in general—something that, given our Puritan culture, many of us are not very skilled at. Finally, there are pencil and paper activities designed to enable you to think about your sexuality and to assess some of your unique needs that can then be communicated to your partner.

For the best results, you will need to devote approximately four 20- to 60-minute blocks of time each week to complete the homework. While the program ideally fits into a three-month period, some couples or individuals who are too busy to carry out the necessary assignments each week will require extra time. It is important that you follow the exercises in order and complete each one successfully before going on to the next set of assignments, even if it means taking a couple of extra weeks to finish the program.

Spending significantly less than the three to four exercise sessions per week may not enable you to generate sufficient momentum to complete the program successfully. Positive experiences are built on positive experiences, but even unsuccessful attempts at the homework assignments offer important lessons in terms of what does not work and the ways in which you may need to fashion your sexual relationship differently.

If there is anything I have learned from 23 years of doing sex therapy and marital counseling, it is that there is no one right way to have a successful intimate and sexual relationship. Each couple must devise for themselves the kind of lovemaking patterns that are the most satisfying for them. The fundamental purpose of following the exercises in this program is to enable you to do precisely that.

For further information, please read *For Yourself: The Fulfillment of Female Sexuality*, which I wrote for women who are not orgasmic with masturbation or *For Each*

Other: Sharing Sexual Intimacy, which I created for women who are consistently orgasmic with masturbation, but not with their partners. These books contain many helpful hints for overcoming a variety of common difficulties you may run into.

Sex is fun. Have a good time with the process. If an exercise doesn't work for you, change it so that it meets your needs more precisely. Again I urge you not to skip any of the exercises. They have all been included for a reason. Each one adds a bit to the totality of new learning that will enable you to have a fully satisfying sexual relationship.

WEEK 1

JOURNAL EXERCISE 1

Keep a journal over the next week in order to record your observations in the following three areas that tend to affect sexual satisfaction:

Feelings about yourself
Feelings about your partner
The explicit sexual contact that takes place

Feelings about yourself

How did you feel about yourself today?
Did you feel attractive or a bit homely?
Were you happy, sad, or angry about something?
Were you tired and under stress? Were you full of energy?
Did you handle some situation particularly well or did some interaction still bother you?

Rate from 1 to 10 (from terrible to great)

Feelings about your partner

Did you feel close to your partner?
Did you feel withdrawn and distant?
Did you feel criticized by your partner?
Did you think of your partner today in a loving way?
Did you have a fight? Did you make up?
Did you have any sexual thoughts regarding your partner?

Rate from 1 to 10 (from distant to close)

Explicit Sexual Contact

Interest and initiation

What led up to sex? How did you feel about that? Who initiated sex? Did that please you? Were you feeling close and affectionate? Or were you preoccupied with other things? Did you feel sexual or would you rather have said no?

Time and place

What time of day did you have sex? If at night, were you tired? If in the morning were you rushed? Were you afraid of disturbing others or of being interrupted? Where did you have sex? Any special preparations?

Sexual activities

Which sexual activities aroused you? Which did not? Was there enough kissing, touching, foreplay? Did you have oral sex? What intercourse position(s) did you use?

Thoughts and fantasies

Did your thoughts or feelings get in the way? Were you worried about your partner's pleasure? Were you concerned whether or not you were a good lover? Concerned about having an orgasm? Were you preoccupied or angry? Did you incorporate any sexual fantasies into lovemaking?

Arousal and satisfaction

Rate both your sexual arousal level and overall satisfaction with each lovemaking session. **Use a scale from 0–10. On the arousal scale: 0 = no arousal, 10 = high arousal. On the satisfaction scale: 0 = high dissatisfaction, 5 = neutral, 10 = high satisfaction.** Notice any patterns?

Keep the journal at your bedside and record your feelings at the end of each day or just after you wake up. Don't wait more than 24 hours to record your feelings; your memory can play tricks on you.

Avoid value judgements. Be careful not to label any behaviors, feelings, or attitudes as good or bad. Just try to note your observations.

SAMPLE JOURNAL ENTRIES

DIARY

DATE: Tues. 1/5
SELF: Rated 10. Felt great—got a raise today!
PARTNER: Rated 9. Bob was very happy for me.
SEXUAL CONTACT:
Time and place: In bed around 11:30 P.M. We spent about an hour together. I was tired by then.
Interest and initiation: I initiated sex and felt very interested.
Sexual activities: I enjoyed having oral sex, but felt anxious as he started to enter me. Missionary position used. No orgasm as usual.
Thoughts and fantasies: Feeling depressed that I'll never have an orgasm with Bob.

Overall arousal = 8 Overall satisfaction = 4

DIARY

DATE: Wed. 1/6
SELF: Rated 7. Generally felt good.
PARTNER: Rated 7. Normal day.
SEXUAL CONTACT:
Time and place: None
Interest and initiation:
Sexual activities:
Thoughts and fantasies:

Overall arousal = Overall satisfaction =

DIARY

DATE: Thurs. 1/7
SELF: Rated 5. Felt kind of ho-hum.
PARTNER: Rated 3. Bob was late for dinner.
SEXUAL CONTACT:
Time and place: In bed—late, around 1 a.m. I was exhausted.
Interest and initiation: Not interested—he initiated.
Sexual activities: Not much foreplay—intercourse was quick.
Thoughts and fantasies: None. Wanted to sleep.

Overall arousal = 2 Overall satisfaction = 2

YOUR JOURNAL ENTRIES

DIARY

DATE: ____________
SELF: ____________
PARTNER: ____________
SEXUAL CONTACT:
Time and place: ____________
Interest and initiation: ____________
Sexual activities: ____________
Thoughts and fantasies: ____________

Overall arousal = Overall satisfaction =

DIARY

DATE: ________________

SELF: ________________

PARTNER: ________________

SEXUAL CONTACT:

Time and place: ________________

Interest and initiation: ________________

Sexual activities: ________________

Thoughts and fantasies: ________________

Overall arousal =

Overall satisfaction =

Day 2

DIARY

DATE: ________________

SELF: ________________

PARTNER: ________________

SEXUAL CONTACT:

Time and place: ________________

Interest and initiation: ________________

Sexual activities: ________________

Thoughts and fantasies: ________________

Overall arousal =

Overall satisfaction =

Day 3

DIARY

DATE: ______________

SELF: ______________

PARTNER: ______________

SEXUAL CONTACT:

Time and place: ______________

Interest and initiation: ______________

Sexual activities: ______________

Thoughts and fantasies: ______________

Overall arousal = Overall satisfaction =

Day 4

DIARY

DATE: ______________

SELF: ______________

PARTNER: ______________

SEXUAL CONTACT:

Time and place: ______________

Interest and initiation: ______________

Sexual activities: ______________

Thoughts and fantasies: ______________

Overall arousal = Overall satisfaction =

Day 5

DIARY

DATE: ________________
SELF: ________________
PARTNER: ________________

SEXUAL CONTACT:

Time and place: ________________

Interest and initiation: ________________

Sexual activities: ________________

Thoughts and fantasies: ________________

Overall arousal =

Overall satisfaction =

Day 6

DIARY

DATE: ________________
SELF: ________________
PARTNER: ________________

SEXUAL CONTACT:

Time and place: ________________

Interest and initiation: ________________

Sexual activities: ________________

Thoughts and fantasies: ________________

Overall arousal =

Overall satisfaction =

Day 7

PLEASURE LIST

Most of us do our work very well—but we've forgotten how to have fun!

Make a list of simple activities that give you pleasure—like this:

1. Watching a favorite TV show
2. Buying flowers
3. Window shopping
4. Taking a long walk
5. Playing a game of tennis
6. Taking time to read the paper
7. Taking a leisurely bath
8. Eating chocolate chip cookies

List at least 10 items—the more, the better!

After you have made your list, carry out a few of the items on it every day for a week! Yes! Every day!

This may seem like an easy exercise but it can be surprisingly difficult for many people.

PLEASURE LIST

1. ____________________
2. ____________________
3. ____________________
4. ____________________
5. ____________________
6. ____________________
7. ____________________
8. ____________________
9. ____________________
10. ____________________

Day 1 ______ ____________________

____

Day 2 ______ ____________________

____

Day 3 ______ ____________________

____

Day 4 ______ ____________________

____

Day 5 ______ ____________________

____

Day 6 ______ ____________________

____

Day 7 ______ ____________________

____

KEGEL EXERCISES FOR WOMEN

These exercises were developed by Dr. Arnold Kegel and help to strengthen and tone the PC or pubococcygeal muscle, which is the main muscle that contracts during orgasm. Regular practice may increase sexual sensations during intercourse and help women achieve stronger and more pleasurable orgasms.

First determine exactly which muscle is the one you need to work with. The correct muscle is the one you squeeze to stop the flow of urine. The next time you are in the bathroom, keep your legs slightly apart and while you are urinating, stop the flow a few times to become familiar with using this muscle.

Squeeze/Release

Start by squeezing and releasing this muscle 5 times, twice a day. Increase by 5 contractions each day until you have worked up to 70 contractions a day (35 during each session).

Squeeze/Hold/Release

As you squeeze the muscle hold for a count of 3 and then release. Once again, begin with 10 contractions a day (5 during each session) and work up to 70 contractions a day (35 during each session).

Flutter

Again, start with 5 contractions each session, but this time squeeze and release as fast as possible. Don't worry if this feels a bit strange at first and you have trouble telling the difference between squeezing and releasing. As you practice, it will become easier. Once again, begin with 10 contractions a day (5 during each session) and work up to 70 (35 during each session).

For best results, continue to do the Kegel exercises for the rest of your life.

KEEP A RECORD OF YOUR PROGRESS WITH THE KEGEL EXERCISES

		Squeeze *Number of Contractions*	**Squeeze/Hold** *Number of Contractions*	**Flutter** *Number of Contractions*
Day 1	1st session	______	______	______
Date______	2nd session	______	______	______
Day 2	1st session	______	______	______
Date______	2nd session	______	______	______
Day 3	1st session	______	______	______
Date______	2nd session	______	______	______
Day 4	1st session	______	______	______
Date______	2nd session	______	______	______
Day 5	1st session	______	______	______
Date______	2nd session	______	______	______
Day 6	1st session	______	______	______
Date______	2nd session	______	______	______
Day 7	1st session	______	______	______
Date______	2nd session	______	______	______
Day 8	1st session	______	______	______
Date______	2nd session	______	______	______

APPRECIATIONS EXERCISE

For one week, take time every day to think of three things that you appreciated about your partner that day. Make sure to tell her or him before the end of the day!

SAMPLE

Jan 6 You made love even though you were tired.
You went to the bank for me.
You called just to say "hi".

Day 1 ______

Day 2 ______

Day 3 ______

Day 4 ______

Day 5 ______

Day 6 ______

Day 7 ______

WEEK 2

SEXUAL SCRIPTING EXERCISE

As we grow up, many of us receive a sexual "script" from our parents and others that strongly influences our attitudes toward sexuality. Now might be the time to change the script to accommodate your present life and suit the grown man or woman you've become. For example, sometimes little girls are taught that sex is bad or little boys are told that masturbation is shameful. These feelings can linger on into adulthood and affect your sex life in negative ways. Take some time to think about your parents' attitudes toward sex, what they told you, and how you felt during these discussions, or how you felt about the lack of them. Try also to think about conversations you have had with friends, or what you have been taught by your religious upbringing.

Note which attitudes you consider positive and want to keep in your script. And note those attitudes that are negative and that you might want to change or drop from your script. Remember, you can direct your own life now!

My Personal History

Positive Attitudes:

____

____

____

____

____

____

Negative Attitudes:

____

____

____

____

____

____

SELF-PORTRAIT

Use a small mirror; look at your genitals. Look at the different shapes, textures and colors of the various parts. See how the different areas look separately and together as a whole.

Spend at least five minutes drawing a picture of your genitals.

Drawing of your genitals:

MIRROR EXERCISE

There are very few people who are completely comfortable with their bodies. Many men are concerned about the size of their penis. Many women think their breasts are too large or too small. But feeling bad about your body can get in the way of enjoying sex. Some things can be changed if they are really important to you. For example, diet and exercise can help if you're serious about getting in shape. But no matter how much you do, there will always be some things that are simply unchangeable. Things that you will have to learn to accept about yourself.

To accept your body, you need to get to know it. To do this, stand in front of a mirror and look carefully at your body from all angles, in all positions. Spend at least 20 minutes. Verbalize what you see as you go along.

This exercise may feel uncomfortable and seem like it takes forever, but since this is the only body you'll ever have—it will be worth it. Feeling good about your body leads to greater freedom when making love.

List three things that you became aware of in a new way as a result of doing the mirror exercise:

1. ____

____

____

2. ____

____

____

3. ____

____

____

CARING DAYS

Make a list of at least 10 things that your partner does, or could do for you that make you feel cared for—then add to the list each day. These should be small things like calling from work, kissing you good-bye, planning a night on the town, complimenting you on how you look. All the items on the list should be positive—what you would like your partner to start to do or continue to do, *not* what you want your partner to stop doing.

Caring Days List

1. ______________________________
2. ______________________________
3. ______________________________
4. ______________________________
5. ______________________________
6. ______________________________
7. ______________________________
8. ______________________________
9. ______________________________
10. ______________________________
11. ______________________________
12. ______________________________
13. ______________________________
14. ______________________________
15. ______________________________
16. ______________________________
17. ______________________________
18. ______________________________

Share your Caring Lists with each other and then post them on the refrigerator door or bathroom mirror as gentle reminders. **Carry out three of the items on your partner's list every day.**

What did you do today to show your partner you care?

Monday

__________ __________ __________

Tuesday

__________ __________ __________

Wednesday

__________ __________ __________

Thursday

__________ __________ __________

Friday

__________ __________ __________

Saturday

__________ __________ __________

Sunday

__________ __________ __________

BAN ON ORGASM

The object of these early exercises is to increase your sexual pleasure. To take off the pressure to respond with orgasm, which actually blocks the arousal process, there will be a ban on orgasm during partner sex until the appropriate partner exercises later in the program. **Do not try to have an orgasm during lovemaking with your partner. Better yet, don't even think about orgasm.** Orgasm, however, may be experienced during the masturbation exercises.

WEEK 3

SAY "NO"

If we don't feel the freedom to say "no" to things that are requested of us we can build up resentment which can spill over and affect our sexual response. When you can say "no" freely and without guilt to those things you don't want to do, you will be able to say "yes" with greater enthusiasm at other times.

Say NO to three things a day that you really don't want to do, but normally would agree to do. You can say NO to a request by someone else. Or you can say NO to yourself when you feel that you "should" be doing something.

List the three things you said NO to each day this week.

Monday

____________ ____________ ____________

Tuesday

____________ ____________ ____________

Wednesday

____________ ____________ ____________

Thursday

____________ ____________ ____________

Friday

____________ ____________ ____________

Saturday

____________ ____________ ____________

Sunday

____________ ____________ ____________

SELF-PLEASURING

Many of us have grown up with negative feelings about masturbation, resulting in a tendency to feel guilty or abnormal if we masturbate. Yet we now know that masturbation is perfectly normal and not in itself at all unhealthy. It is practiced by most people of both sexes and can teach us a lot about becoming orgasmic.

One of the best ways to learn about yourself and to change your sexual patterns is through masturbation, because you can do it in complete privacy and at your own pace. You don't have to worry about how you look or your partner's response and, since you get immediate feedback, the learning can occur more quickly.

Pick the appropriate masturbation assignments:

(A) Women who are unable to masturbate to orgasm using their hands

(B) Women who are reliably orgasmic with manual masturbation, but never or rarely with partner sex

(C) Women who have been orgasmic with previous partners, but not with their current partners

(D) Women who used to be orgasmic with their current partners, but are not any longer

(E) Women who are inconsistently orgasmic with their partners

BEGINNING TOUCH

(A) For Women Who Have Never Been Orgasmic with Manual Masturbation

Set aside *one full hour* when you will have no interruptions. Find a place that is private and warm enough so that you will be comfortable while nude. First get into the right erotic frame of mind. You might want to remember a past sexual encounter that was very exciting for you, or make up a fantasy of your own. Try reading an erotic book. Look at a book of sensual photographs. Watch an erotic video. **Once you have been aroused mentally, begin to touch yourself. Start with light strokes all over your body. Experiment. Try different touches and different positions—lie on your back, your side or stomach. When you feel relaxed and comfortable begin touching your breasts, then your genitals.**

You may find that using oil or some other lubricant enhances your enjoyment. Most women stimulate their clitoris or labia during masturbation.

Again experiment with different touches and strokes. Try up-and-down strokes, side-to-side strokes, or circular motions. Vary them as you reach different levels of arousal—or whenever you desire. Don't feel discouraged if you masturbate for a while and nothing seems to be happening. It takes time to learn to tune into your body's needs and desires. Try just to become aware of the different sensations and the ones you particularly enjoy. Repeat this exercise until you are comfortable touching and giving pleasure to yourself. Write down your observations on the following page.

What Turned You On?

EXAMPLE

Date	Mental Stimulation	Physical Stimulation
1/20	Fantasy of last New Year's Eve	Alternate between firm & light touch

WEEK 3

	Date	Mental Stimulation	Physical Stimulation
1	________	________	________
		________	________
2	________	________	________
		________	________
3	________	________	________
		________	________
4	________	________	________
		________	________
5	________	________	________
		________	________
6	________	________	________
		________	________

COMPARING MASTURBATION WITH PARTNER SEX

(B) For Women Who Are Orgasmic with Manual Masturbation but Rarely Experience Orgasm with a Partner

To observe your masturbation pattern more carefully and see how it compares to lovemaking with your partner, set up a sensual atmosphere and prolong the stimulation. Even if it usually takes you just a couple of minutes to masturbate to orgasm, slow down the experience so that it lasts 30 minutes to one hour in order to pay close attention to the process.

For example: If you masturbate on your stomach, see if you are generally on your back during partners sex. Or, if you use hard direct clitoral stimulation with masturbation, notice if the stimulation you receive from your partner is lighter or less direct.

Observe your masturbation pattern and your lovemaking with your partner twice each.

List of Masturbation Turn-ons	How They Compare with Partner Sex
EXAMPLE Start out with breast stimulation.	He goes right for genitals.
1. ______________________	______________________
2. ______________________	______________________
3. ______________________	______________________
4. ______________________	______________________
5. ______________________	______________________
6. ______________________	______________________
7. ______________________	______________________
8. ______________________	______________________

EROTIC STYLES

(C) For Women Who Have Been Orgasmic with Previous Partners but Are Not with Their Current Partners

Write down a short description of your partner's sexual technique. Write as though you were describing him for an erotic magazine. Include his style of lovemaking, choice of touches, way of kissing, speed, and attitudes. Is he serious? Playful? Romantic?

Now write about the technique of the partner(s) you have been orgasmic with. Compare the two descriptions.

Your current partner's sexual techniques

____

____

____

____

Previous partner(s) sexual techniques

____

____

____

____

Ways they are different

____

____

____

____

SEXUAL CLUES

(D) For Women Who Used to Be Orgasmic with Their Current Partners

Make a timetable of you and your partner's history together. Try to remember when you first noticed that you were no longer reaching an orgasm with your partner. On the following pages write down where you lived and what was happening in your life, where you made love, and what your sex life was like. Try to visualize your surroundings and relive in your mind the sexual experiences that took place starting about two months before your orgasms ceased, noting which experiences ended in orgasm and which didn't.

The point is to approximate when the orgasms stopped. Was it sudden or did they go away gradually? **Once you can pinpoint the time your orgasms stopped occurring you will be better able to zero in on the cause.** Try to think if some particular event or emotional upset occurred at that time.

SEXUAL CLUES

Approximate date when you realized that you were becoming less orgasmic with your partner ____________________

Recall a sexual event approximately two months prior to this date.

Where did you make love? ____________________

Were you orgasmic? ____________________

Any relevant insights? ____________________

____

____

Recall a sexual event approximately one month prior to this date.

Where did you make love? ____________________

Were you orgasmic? ____________________

Any relevant insights? ____________________

____

____

Recall a sexual event around the date that you first noticed you were not as orgasmic with your partner.

Where did you make love? ____________________

Were you orgasmic? ____________________

Any relevant insights? ____________________

____

____

If you have been with your partner for many years, you may want to explore the period from six months to one year prior to the date when you first noticed there was a problem.

JOURNAL EXERCISE 2

(E) For Women Who Are Inconsistently Orgasmic with Their Partners

If you are orgasmic with your partner, but not often enough, repeat the Journal Exercise from Week 1, paying special attention to those sexual experiences that resulted in orgasm.

How did you feel about yourself before making love? How did you feel about your partner? What time of day did you make love? Did you want to make love? Where did you make love? How much time did you spend? What sexual activities did you engage in? Notice any patterns that discriminate between whether or not you are likely to have an orgasm?

Fill in after each sexual experience.

Day 1

Feelings about yourself ______________________________

Feelings toward your partner ______________________________

Time of day for lovemaking ______________________________

Location ______________________________

Time spent ______________________________

Activities engaged in ______________________________

Other ______________________________

Arousal level ______________________________

Satisfaction level ______________________________

Did you have an orgasm?_____Yes _____No

Day 2

Feelings about yourself ______________________________

Feelings toward your partner ______________________________

Time of day for lovemaking ______________________________

Location ______________________________

Time spent ______________________________

Activities engaged in ______________________________

Other ______________________________

Arousal level ______________________________

Satisfaction level ______________________________

Did you have an orgasm?_____Yes _____No

Day 3
Feelings about yourself ______________________________

Feelings toward your partner ______________________________

Time of day for lovemaking ______________________________

Location ______________________________

Time spent ______________________________

Activities engaged in ______________________________

Other ______________________________

Arousal level ______________________________

Satisfaction level ______________________________

Did you have an orgasm?_____Yes _____No

Day 4
Feelings about yourself ______________________________

Feelings toward your partner ______________________________

Time of day for lovemaking ______________________________

Location ______________________________

Time spent ______________________________

Activities engaged in ______________________________

Other ______________________________

Arousal level ______________________________

Satisfaction level ______________________________

Did you have an orgasm?_____Yes _____No

What patterns do you notice?
I'm unlikely to have an orgasm if ______________________________

____

____

____

____

I'm likely to have an orgasm if ______________________________

____

____

____

____

CARING MASSAGE

A caring massage is a pleasurable way to explore intimacy. It is not sexual, but an opportunity to get close and enjoy being together. The object is to soothe and relax, not to work out muscle kinks.

Prepare a comfortable environment where you won't be disturbed. Create your own world—just for the two of you. It doesn't have to be elaborate. Find a quiet room, close the shades, add some flowers, light a candle or two. Lie on the rug or on a firm mattress freshly made up with attractive sheets. Anywhere that you feel warm, comfortable, and secure will do. And don't forget a spill-proof bottle of oil; it's essential for a good massage. The oil should have a light, pleasant scent that you both enjoy.

Make sure you have everything you need—once you start you won't want to be interrupted.

As Giver: Spend 30 minutes experiencing and stroking your partner's body in a loving way that gives *you* pleasure. Don't emphasize breasts and genitals, but don't avoid them either.

As Receiver: Relax and enjoy the massage. If a certain kind of touching feels unpleasant to you, let your partner know in a positive way how it could be changed: For example, "A little more firmly, please—that tickles." If the touch is neutral or positive, simply relax and enjoy it.

After 30 minutes switch roles. Repeat this exercise on two separate occasions.

First Massage

Role as Giver: What you learned from doing the exercise

___

___

Role as Receiver: What you learned from doing the exercise

___

___

Second Massage

Role as Giver: What you learned from doing the exercise

___

___

Role as Receiver: What you learned from doing the exercise

___

___

WEEK 4

SAY "YES"

Say YES to yourself. Ask for, or let yourself have three things a day that you would really like to have. Make sure these are things you would not normally let yourself have or ask for. Begin small: Ask for help with a job you would normally do yourself, or treat yourself to a small gift, or 15 minutes in the sun.

If you feel guilty when doing this exercise—ignore that feeling!

Don't worry if you find yourself getting confused as to whether you are doing the "Yes" or "No" exercise. They're opposite sides of the same coin.

List the three things you said YES to each day this week.

Monday

__________ __________ __________

Tuesday

__________ __________ __________

Wednesday

__________ __________ __________

Thursday

__________ __________ __________

Friday

__________ __________ __________

Saturday

__________ __________ __________

Sunday

__________ __________ __________

MASTURBATION EXERCISES

Do the **Intensified Touch** masturbation exercise if you are not orgasmic with masturbation using your hand. Otherwise complete the **Varying Your Masturbation Pattern** exercise.

INTENSIFIED TOUCH

(A) For Women Who Have Never Been Orgasmic with Masturbation or a Partner

This exercise is similar to the first masturbation exercise except the duration and the intensity of the stimulation will be increased. Once against, set aside an hour where you will have no interruptions. Find a place that is private and warm enough so that you will be comfortable while nude. Get into the right erotic frame of mind. Take what you have learned about the touching you like and begin touching yourself in a way that you know gives you pleasure. First all over your body, and then concentrating on the genitals. Keep your attention on the sensations of pleasure or on a fantasy that increases your arousal. **Build to a high level of arousal. If the sensations become too intense or uncomfortable, stop the stimulation for a minute and let the sensations subside.** Then begin stimulating yourself again. Stop again if the sensations become too intense, but push to a higher intensity than you reached before stopping the first time. Continue this process of reaching higher and higher levels of arousal until orgasm naturally occurs. Do not expect this to happen the first or second time you carry out this exercise. Some women find it takes a few weeks of daily practice.

If you have completed this exercise a number of times and are reaching high levels of arousal, but feel you need a little boost to go over the top to orgasm, consider massaging your clitoris with a vibrator. You can place the vibrator directly on your clitoris or put your hand or a towel on top of your clitoris and then place the vibrator over it. Once you have experienced an orgasm with vibrator stimulation, repeat the exercise, at a separate time, but use only your hands. Repeat this exercise as often as necessary until you have experienced an orgasm with manual stimulation. Then go on to the next masturbation exercise, Varying Your Masturbation Pattern, before going on to Week 5.

Descriptions of Orgasm

Some women find it difficult to identify an orgasm. The following are signposts:

- A rise in the intensity of sexual sensation that seems to peak for a moment and then rapidly falls to a lower level of arousal.

- Muscles around the opening of your vagina tighten and contract during a moment of intensity (You can feel this if you put your finger inside the vagina.)

- Your clitoris becomes extremely sensitive following a feeling of warmth or release.

While the above are some physical indications that you may have reached an orgasm, the following emotional feelings are just as important, but may not be true for women who are multi-orgasmic:

- A feeling of relaxation

- Feelings of satisfaction and completion

- No immediate desire for further sexual stimulation

Don't expect to experience all of these signs. One or two are fine. After all, every woman's response is unique. **Record your observations on the following page.**

INTENSIFIED TOUCH

What turned you on and how turned on were you?
0 = no arousal to 10 = orgasm

EXAMPLE

Date	Mental Stimulation	Physical Stimulation	Rating
Jan 6	Reading *Fanny Hill*	Circular strokes on head of clitoris; squeezing thigh muscles together	3

	Date	Mental Stimulation	Physical Stimulation	Rating
1	________	________	________	________
2	________	________	________	________
3	________	________	________	________
4	________	________	________	________
5	________	________	________	________
6	________	________	________	________
7	________	________	________	________
8	________	________	________	________

VARYING YOUR MASTURBATION PATTERN

(B–E) For Women Who Are Orgasmic with Manual Masturbation

You can learn to be more responsive to partner stimulation by broadening your masturbation pattern. **Set aside an hour to try masturbating in new ways.** Begin by fantasizing or by reading or watching erotica to get mentally aroused. Then, if you usually lie on your back, try masturbating on your stomach. If you usually use your right hand, try your left. Substitute firm stimulation if you generally use a light touch. If your legs are usually together, try spreading them apart, etc. Expect it to take much longer to reach orgasm when you break away from your tried and true pattern, but don't let this worry you. Slowly you will be teaching yourself to respond to new kinds of stimulation.

Repeat this exercise until you feel you have learned all you can from it but repeat it at least three times.

EXAMPLE

Date	**New Techniques Tried**
Jan 11	Masturbating on side Up and down strokes instead of circular strokes Used right hand

Date	**New Techniques Tried**
________	________________________________
	________________________________
	________________________________
________	________________________________
	________________________________
	________________________________
________	________________________________
	________________________________
	________________________________
________	________________________________
	________________________________
	________________________________

SENSUAL MASSAGE

A sensual massage can be an extremely erotic addition to your lovemaking. The combination of relaxation and arousal is hard to beat. So as you did with the Caring Massage, prepare a comfortable environment where you won't be disturbed. Sharing a refreshing shower together is sometimes a nice way to begin.

For this massage, you can spend a disproportionate amount of time on breasts, genitals and other sexually sensitive areas—but not before spending ample time on the rest of your partner's body.

Switch roles after 30 minutes or longer. Repeat this exercise on two separate occasions. (Remember, the ban on orgasm during partner sex is still in effect.)

First Massage

Role as Giver: What you learned from doing the exercise

____

____

____

Role as Receiver: What you learned from doing the exercise

____

____

____

Second Massage

Role as Giver: What you learned from doing the exercise

____

____

____

Role as Receiver: What you learned from doing the exercise

____

____

____

RESISTANCE

As you begin to make changes you may notice that you start to feel afraid. While consciously you may be convinced that you do not want things to stay the same, there is always a certain amount of fear of the unknown; the fear that if things change, they could become worse. If, and when, the fears start to win out over the desire to grow, you may neglect to do the homework, or feel that the assignments are irrelevant, or pick fights with your partner that make working on the problem impossible. But stick with it.

I cannot stress enough that you *will* feel discouraged along the way if real changes are being made. Don't let it get you down. Here are some ideas that will help you get back on track:

- If you need to, take off a day or two days at most.

- Repeat some of the earlier exercises that were carried out successfully as a way of bolstering your confidence.

- Do the exercises for this week a second time. Suspend any negative judgements or feelings of failure. This is a process. The time-line will vary from woman to woman. Success is the result of tenacity. If you stick with the process, you *will* be successful.

- Use your own creativity. Create variations on the exercises to make them more relevant or appealing to you.

WEEK 5

ENJOY THE MOMENT

For this exercise, it's helpful to have a watch with an alarm function. If you're at home use an alarm clock or a kitchen timer. Set your watch or timer to alert you once every hour.

Every time the alarm rings, stop and think of what you are doing at that very moment. How are you feeling? Could you add anything to the activity you are performing that would give you greater pleasure? Eating a meal slowly, for instance, and savoring every bite. Enjoying the wind in your hair as you take a walk. Even doing a job you don't like in the most efficient way possible so that you'll be finished more quickly.

Notice your enjoyment level for one day and evening. The purpose of this exercise is to help you to focus on the pleasure of the moment and how to get the most out of it.

Activity	How did you make it more pleasurable?

AFFIRMATIONS

Often our concept of sex has been colored by parental disapproval and other negative attitudes. This creates an inner voice that says that sex is bad. As we listen to this voice, we are constantly scripting ourselves for failure.

To counteract this voice, **write each of the following affirmations at least once a day for the next week** (preferaby two or three times each day). After you have written them, read them back to yourself, first silently and then out loud.

Sex is a natural way for me to share myself with my partner.

I feel safe to act on my sexual desires.

I love being a sexy woman and deserve the pleasure I get from making love with my mate.

Now make up one or two affirmations of your own.

For the next week, silently repeat all of these affirmations to yourself before making love with your partner.

Write down three to four affirmations each day:

Day 1: Date ________

1. ______________________________

____

2. ______________________________

____

3. ______________________________

____

4. ______________________________

____

Day 2: Date ________

1. ______________________________

____

2. ______________________________

____

3. ______________________________

____

4. ______________________________

____

Day 3: Date ________

1. ______________________________

____

2. ______________________________

____

3. ______________________________

____

4. ______________________________

____

Day 4: Date ________

1. ______________________________

____

2. ______________________________

____

3. ______________________________

____

4. ______________________________

____

Day 5: Date ________

1. ______________________________

____

2. ______________________________

____

3. ______________________________

____

4. ______________________________

____

Day 6: Date ________

1. ______________________________

____

2. ______________________________

____

3. ______________________________

____

4. ______________________________

____

Day 7: Date ________

1. ______________________________

____

2. ______________________________

____

3. ______________________________

____

4. ______________________________

____

Which affirmation was most effective for you?

____

Which affirmation was least effective for you?

Why?

Rewrite your least effective affirmation in a way that is more helpful to you—try using the phrase "I am learning to . . ."

For example, you would rewrite "I love being a sexy woman" to "I am learning to love being a sexy woman"

BODY-LOVE EXERCISE

Expanding Orgasmic Potential for all Women

Most women consider masturbation a purely genital experience. They rarely include stimulation of other parts of their bodies—the neck, the breasts, or the inner thighs, for example. **In this exercise, masturbate as a way of making love to yourself rather than merely striving for the orgasm.** Go slowly and massage and touch different parts of your body in a way that you enjoy. Don't touch your genitals until you have stroked your breasts, stomach, thighs, and buttocks. Only then, proceed to the clitoris or vaginal area.

Repeat this exercise until you think you have learned all you can from it.

Date **What you discovered**

________ ____

____

____

________ ____

____

____

________ ____

____

____

________ ____

____

____

CONDITIONS FOR GOOD SEX

Make a list of those things that make a sexual experience good for you. Ask your partner to make a similar list.

A few examples:

- Taking your time
- Oral sex
- Not being too tired
- Hard stimulation of your penis/gentle clitoral stroking
- A massage
- Certain music
- Soft lighting

Let this list be as long as you like—but make sure that you write down at least 10 items!

1. ______________________________
2. ______________________________
3. ______________________________
4. ______________________________
5. ______________________________
6. ______________________________
7. ______________________________
8. ______________________________
9. ______________________________
10. ______________________________

WEEK 6

INTENSIFYING ORGASM

Masturbate in a way you enjoy that produces strong feelings of arousal. As you get close to an orgasm find ways to reduce the sensations somewhat so that you keep yourself at the edge of orgasm. As your level of excitement lowers, stimulate yourself once again until you are very close to orgasm. Do this three or four times, then build the intensity as much as possible while holding back your orgasm until the last possible second.

Repeat this exercise until you think you have learned all you can from it.

Date **What you discovered:**

_________ ______________________________

____

____

_________ ______________________________

____

____

_________ ______________________________

____

____

_________ ______________________________

____

____

SHARING "CONDITIONS FOR GOOD SEX" LISTS

Last week you each made a list of those things that are most likely to make a sexual experience more enjoyable for you. Since everyone is different, you cannot possibly know everything your partner needs for a good sexual experience and your partner cannot automatically know what you need.

Share your Conditions for Good Sex lists to convey your sexual needs to each other. Talking explicitly about your sexual needs may provide new information for your partner. You may find that you've been touching your partner the way *you* would like to be touched as a way of communicating *your* preferences. Your partner, on the other hand, may be doing the same with you. Perhaps your preferences are quite different. Talking about them will go a long way toward clearing up the nonverbal *mis*communication.

CONDITIONS FOR GOOD SEX

Conditions that are different

For example: I like sex at night/partner likes sex in the morning.

1. ______________________
2. ______________________
3. ______________________
4. ______________________
5. ______________________
6. ______________________
7. ______________________

Conditions that you share

For example: We both prefer lots of time.

1. ______________________
2. ______________________
3. ______________________
4. ______________________
5. ______________________
6. ______________________
7. ______________________

Now brainstorm to add more items to the shared list.

8. ______________________
9. ______________________
10. ______________________
11. ______________________
12. ______________________

WEEK 7

"I" MESSAGES

One of the most important communication skills to learn is the use of "I" messages.

Begin to use the words "I feel" when talking with your partner.

For example, "*I* feel unimportant when you're late for dinner and don't call," is much more effective than, "*You* don't care about anyone but yourself, or you wouldn't keep me waiting."

The "You" statement is a blaming statement, and will often start or escalate an argument.

An "I" statement reports your feelings and generally makes it easier for your partner to respond in a positive way.

Feelings are expressed by such words as: hurt, frustrated, lonely, inadequate, happy, loving.

Think of something your partner did that upset you and write how it made you feel—as if you were telling your partner at the time.

I feel ____________________ when you do/say ________________________________

____

Beware: Don't use "I feel" when you mean "I think." "I feel *that* you ..." or "I feel *as* though you ..." or "I feel *like* you ..." are thinking statements, not feeling statements. You are analyzing your partner, not expressing your feelings.

Think of something else your partner did that upset you and write how it made you feel—as if you were telling your partner at the time:

I feel ____________________ when you do/say ________________________________

____

COMMUNICATING PREFERENCES

Each person has unique sexual preferences. Your partner is not a mind reader. The purpose of this exercise is to let your partner know as much as possible about your sexual likes and dislikes.

Compile a list of all the ways you enjoy being touched. Be as specific as possible. For example: "I like to begin with light touches all over my body; I love my hair pulled as I get more excited," and so on. Whenever possible, state each item in the list in a positive way. Rather than listing, "I don't like direct clitoral stimulation right away," write, "I like clitoral stimulation best after I'm warmed up a bit."

At the same time, make a list of all the sexual touches and activities you *think* your partner enjoys most. Then read each other's list and discuss each item in detail.

List the ways you enjoy being touched sexually.

____

____

____

____

____

____

____

____

____

____

____

____

List the ways you think your partner enjoys being touched during sex.

What did you both learn when you discussed your lists?

ASKING FANTASY

Mentally review your masturbation assignments and your Communicating Preferences list as well as other pertinent exercises in order to discover what is important in order for you to experience orgasm.

Now fantasize that you are making love with your partner as you masturbate in any way that gives you pleasure.

During the fantasy, imagine asking your partner for the types of strokes, kisses, oral sex, and so on that you prefer.

While you go through the lovemaking scene in your imagination, don't feel under any pressure to achieve an orgasm. Just try to connect your fantasy with pleasurable feelings.

Carry out this assignment in fantasy five or six times until you feel comfortable enough with the process to try it in real life.

List some things that would make sex better for you:

1. ______________________________

2. ______________________________

3. ______________________________

4. ______________________________

5. ______________________________

Date	What did you imagine asking for or initiating in your fantasy?
________	______________________________
	______________________________
________	______________________________
	______________________________
________	______________________________
	______________________________
________	______________________________
	______________________________

WEEK 8

ACTIVE LISTENING

When a disagreement comes up, most of us don't really listen to our partners because we are too busy preparing our own replies. To prevent this, try this simple exercise: Pick a topic that has caused a moderate amount of conflict in your relationship. Both partners should limit their statements to just a few sentences at a time. The person listening must feed back to the partner what he or she just heard the partner say before presenting his or her own point of view.

Both partners switch back and forth in this manner:

1. *He* makes a short statement expressing his point of view.
2. *She* repeats what she heard him say.
3. *He* agrees with her translation or corrects it.
4. Once she has repeated it back to his satisfaction, *she* succinctly states *her* own point of view. (*He* then repeats it as in 2, and so forth.)

Try "active listening" four times, alternating who picks the issue to discuss.

Date	Topic of discussion	What you learned about your partner's point of view
______	______	______
	______	______
		______
______	______	______
	______	______
		______
______	______	______
	______	______
		______
______	______	______
	______	______
		______

FOREPLAY

An important cause of lack of orgasm can be insufficient time spent during foreplay. Most women require *at least* 20 minutes of foreplay before beginning intercourse in order to experience orgasm.

For this exercise set aside a full hour to make love with your partner. You might want to choose a time earlier in the evening or some morning or afternoon when you have no other plans. **Take time for whatever you really enjoy—kissing, massage, or oral sex. The only activity that is off-limits is intercourse.** Touch, taste and explore every part of your bodies together. Give voice to one or two of the things you imagined asking for in last week's Asking Fantasy or Communicating Preferences exercise. Share fantasies if you like. The purpose of this exercise is to heighten arousal only—so relax and enjoy this time together. If orgasm happens that's fine, but that is not the point of this exercise. In fact, try to prevent yourself from reaching orgasm for at least the first 40 minutes. Just fully explore the pleasure that extended foreplay provides.

Date	What foreplay activities did you expand on?
________	____
	____
	____
________	____
	____
	____
________	____
	____
	____

WEEK 9

ALWAYS/NEVER EXERCISE

Discontinue using the words NEVER and ALWAYS. As in, "You're *always* late" or "You *never* help me with the dishes." The problem with using these words is that your partner will focus on the exceptions and the point you are trying to make will be lost.

Most important, it is necessary to remember that the object is not to win the argument. If one person wins the other loses, and then both lose, because the loser will find some way to get even. Instead, the object is to understand your partner's point of view, to hear what his or her needs are and to take responsibility for whatever your part was in the conflict. This makes it easier to reconcile and let go. In the end it's a lot more fun to feel loving and close. Hard feelings and emotional distance are just plain painful.

For three days try to keep track of how many times you say "always" or "never" to your partner. Aim for zero.

Day 1	**Number of times you said "always"**	**Number of times you said "never"**
Morning	____________	____________
Afternoon	____________	____________
Evening	____________	____________
TOTAL	____________	____________
Day 2		
Morning	____________	____________
Afternoon	____________	____________
Evening	____________	____________
TOTAL	____________	____________
Day 3		
Morning	____________	____________
Afternoon	____________	____________
Evening	____________	____________
TOTAL	____________	____________

SELF-STIMULATION WITH PARTNER

The purpose of this exercise is to stimulate your clitoris yourself during foreplay with your partner. For this exercise, make love as usual. When you are comfortable, let your hand glide over your breasts and down to your stomach. Take time to enjoy the sensations of touching these soft sensual areas. When you are comfortable—and it doesn't have to be this first session—let your hand go lower still until you reach your clitoris. Stimulate yourself in a way that you know gives you pleasure. The first time you try this, don't worry about having an orgasm. It may take several sessions before you are able to accomplish this. Also, it will probably take you longer to reach an orgasm this way than it does when you masturbate by yourself.

You may want to maintain clitoral stimulation after the point at which your partner ejaculates. In fact, you may feel more able to relax and concentrate on your own orgasm after your partner has had his.

Repeat this exercise until you are confident that you can reach orgasm during intercourse with the aid of self-stimulation.

Date	What you learned from doing this exercise
________	________________________________
	________________________________
	________________________________
________	________________________________
	________________________________
	________________________________
________	________________________________
	________________________________
	________________________________

WEEK 10

PARTNER STIMULATION

The purpose of this exercise is to teach your partner how to stimulate your clitoris. This is more difficult than just doing it yourself. So, in addition to explaining the kind of stimulation you like, it may be helpful to show him. Place yourself in a position that allows your partner to hold and caress you while still being able to clearly observe you. Now begin to stimulate yourself in the ways you enjoy. Try not to feel self-conscious. Actually, the odds are that your partner will feel turned on by watching you. After you've taken about 5 minutes to show him what you like, ask him to try.

Don't worry about having an orgasm, especially the first few times you try this. Just try to teach your partner to stimulate your genitals in a way that gives you pleasure.

Date	What you learned from doing this exercise
________	____
	____
	____
________	____
	____
	____
________	____
	____
	____

EROTIC VIDEOS

If you have a video cassette player, set a date when you and your partner can have some private time to rent an erotic film and watch it together. If you don't have a VCR, think about going to see an erotic film in a theater. With a sense of fun, you can turn it into an adventure. Also, don't worry if the film does not turn you on. Even if it doesn't arouse you or is just amusing, you may notice that you feel more passionate or sexually creative when you make love after watching it.

Date	What you learned from doing the exercise
________	____
________	____
________	____
________	____

Some good erotic videos:

By Erotic Escapades Presents:
Cabin Fever
The Voyeur
The Hottest Bid

By Femme Productions:
Urban Heat
Three Daughters
Christine's Secret

WEEK 11

STATE OF THE UNION EXERCISE

Set aside an hour to talk with your partner about your relationship. Share your feelings on the positive and negative aspects of the preceding week. You may want to talk about specific exercises from this program or other ways you've thought of to spice up your sex life.

End the discussion by letting your partner know three things that he or she did for you during the previous week that you particularly appreciated.

Schedule a "State of the Union" appointment for the next week. This exercise should be carried out every week until it becomes an integral part of your relationship.

Meeting Date ___________________ Time ______________

Negative aspects of preceding week ____

____

____

Positive aspects of preceding week ____

____

____

Three things you appreciated about your partner this past week

____

____

____

Three things your partner appreciated about you this past week

____

____

____

Next meeting:

Date _______________ Time ________________

CLITORAL STIMULATION DURING INTERCOURSE

The purpose of this exercise is to experience orgasm during intercourse by assuming an intercourse position which allows for direct manual clitoral stimulation. The spoon position or women astride position both tend to work well.

Be sure to take sufficient time to build your arousal to a high level before beginning intercourse. Then either you or your partner can stimulate your clitoris while you are having intercourse. Maintain the clitoral stimulation during the entire time you are having intercourse, but don't expect to have an orgasm the first time you carry out this exericse.

Date	What you learned from doing this exercise
________	____
	____
	____
________	____
	____
	____
________	____
	____
	____

INITIATING SEX

Break out of the routine with each partner taking the opportunity to initiate sex in a new and different way.

- Wake your partner up in the middle of the night with a sexual caress.
- Make a secret plan for the children to spend the night with their grandparents or a special friend. Then seduce your partner.
- Leave a sexual invitation on your partner's personal voicemail or in a note folded within his/her clean underwear.
- Park the car in a secluded spot and revisit teenage years.

A little originality goes a long way in creating great sex.

In which new way did *you* initiate sex?________________________________

____

In which new way did *your partner* initiate sex?________________________

____

WEEK 12

G-SPOT STIMULATION

The purpose of this exercise is to provide direct stimulation of the G-spot during intercourse. The G-spot is a small area inside your vagina on the front wall, just about 2 inches from the entrance. Some women find it very arousing to be stimulated in this area, particularly when combined with clitoral stimulation.

Before you begin, let your partner know what position you would prefer. Many women find rear-entry positions best for stimulation of the G-spot. Try getting on your hands and knees, or lie on your stomach or side. Arching your back may increase the sensations. Experiment with other positions as well, such as sitting on your partner's lap.

Once you start making love, make sure that you take enough time to build up your level of arousal before you start actual intercourse. When you do, focus on the sensations you feel in this "G-spot" area, but do not hesitate to add extra clitoral stimulation either with your hand or your partner's hand.

Repeat this exercise as often as you like to determine what positions give you the greatest pleasure.

Date **What you learned from doing this exercise**

________ ____

____

____

________ ____

____

____

________ ____

____

____

________ ____

____

____

TRY SOMETHING NEW

Don't let the day go by without trying to add at least one new thing to your love life. It can be as simple as kissing your lover somewhere you never have before—on the neck or inner thigh. Or as elaborate as designing an evening with all the props you can find—from satin sheets to sex toys. Read to each other; play with each other; talk to each other; act out a fantasy. A good sexual relationship requires time, planning, and preparation. Love and intimacy can grow stale when taken for granted. When was the last time you said, "I love you"?

What did you add to your love life this week?

Monday: ______________________________

Tuesday: ______________________________

Wednesday: ______________________________

Thursday: ______________________________

Friday: ______________________________

Saturday: ______________________________

Sunday: ______________________________

BACKSLIDING

If you've experienced significant positive changes, don't be alarmed when some backsliding takes place from time to time. **It is important to realize that a certain amount of backsliding is a natural part of any growth process.** Your sexuality may be a sensitive area and particularly susceptible to outside stresses or especially vulnerable to difficult periods in your relationship. By keeping your sexual relationship prioritized, backsliding is less likely to occur. If it does, simply repeat the series of exercises that have been most helpful to you.

List the exercises that have been most beneficial for you:

____

____

____

____

____

____

____

____

ACKNOWLEDGMENTS

Many of the sexual exercises have been adapted from *FOR YOURSELF: THE FULFILLMENT OF FEMALE SEXUALITY* or *FOR EACH OTHER: SHARING SEXUAL INTIMACY*, both written by Lonnie Barbach, Ph.D.

CONDITIONS FOR GREAT SEX was developed by Bernie Zilbergeld, Ph.D., author of *THE NEW MALE SEXUALITY*.

FOREPLAY and STATE OF THE UNION come from *GOING THE DISTANCE: FINDING AND KEEPING LIFELONG LOVE* by Lonnie Barbach, Ph.D. and David Geisinger, Ph.D.

CARING DAYS is borrowed from the work of Richard Stuart, D.S.W.

Thanks to Claudia Vagt for her help with the writing and editing of many of the exercises and to Marilyn Anderson for her assistance in organizing and typing the manuscript.